YOUR 7-DAY JOURNEY

TO LOVING YOUR WIFE

For Better or for Worse

Willie G. Miller Jr.

Book design by Victoria Valentine / www.PageAndCoverDesign.com

Proverbs 18:22

He who finds a wife finds a good thing,
and obtains favor from the Lord.

Beverley, thank you for being nice, wonderful,
and right for me. I am truly blessed and
favored by God to have someone who breathes
life into me and causes me to dream.
I love you, over and over again!

Table of Contents

v   **Welcome**

1   **Introduction**

5   **DAY 1: The Commandment**

6   Reflection 1: Self-Sacrificing Love

7   Reflection 2: A Measure for Long-Suffering

9   **DAY 2: Vulnerability**

10 Reflection 3: Service Your Wife Without Regard to Your Vulnerability

11 Reflection 4: Vulnerability is an Inside Job

15 **DAY 3: One Flesh! – What About The Rest?**

17 Reflection 5: To Commune or Not to Commune

21 Reflection 6: Spiritual Oneness

22 Reflection 7: Soul Mates

25 **DAY 4: Looking Inward - Putting On Big Boy Pants**

26 Reflection 8: Husbands Have No License to Withhold Love

28 Reflection 9: Forgive as You Have Been Forgiven

31 Reflection 10: You Did Not Sacrifice Much – Why Should it Cost so Much for Your Forgiveness?

33 **DAY 5: Incomprehensible Love of God / Husband**

34 Reflection 11: The Back Burner Pre/Post Test

39 Reflection 12: No Love for Yourself = No Love for Your Wife

41 Reflection 13: Identity Crisis – Moving from Loving Me to Loving We [Me]

49 **DAY 6: Communication**

53 Reflection 14: Convey Acceptance

58 Reflection 15: Conveying Commitment – Longevity

61 Reflection 16: Convey Gratitude

63 Reflection 17: Conveying Inseparability

67 **DAY 7: The Wrap-Up: What I Learned...**

69 Thank you for taking this journey with me

Welcome

Hello and welcome to *Your 7-Day Journey to Loving Your Wife for Better or for Worse!*

This *7-Day Journey* Workbook was designed to help you strengthen your marriage and build a stronger intimate relationship with your wife in just seven days. As you embark on this journey, I pray your understanding of the mystical relationship that exists between God and the Church [His bride] is increased and that you learn how His example of love can be applied to your relationship with your wife.

This workbook comprises seven sections. Each section represents a day, with two to four reflections each day. The reflections and reading for each day should take about 20–30 minutes depending on how long it takes you to work through the reflective exercises. I highly recommend that after you have completed the entire workbook, you re-visit your answers periodically to evaluate how your relationship is progressing in these areas. Repeat sections as needed.

It is my hope that you use this tool to increase the intimacy in your marriage. While completing the reflective exercises, I ask that you really take time to think through your responses and be completely honest with yourself and God.

I wish you the best and hope that this workbook empowers you with the knowledge and tools to love your wife for better – for worse!

Introduction

The wedding day is here. What an emotional time. We made it through the courting process and here we stand in the presence of God, our family, and friends to openly proclaim our love and commitment to each other and to God. We have all of the best intentions as we look into each other's eyes and vow to each other and to God that we are going to stay together until death do us part, through sickness and health, keeping ourselves solely to the other. After the open show of affection and the public proclamation, we embark on the mystical journey to make our marriage work.

Some marriages last through all of the challenges that are almost guaranteed to come. The challenges are always tailored and specific to the individuals in each relationship. The broad categories are not new; the characters however, are. It does not matter if it is your first, second or third marriage, each time you say I do, you say it to a different person. This holds true even if it is the same person because we evolve as peo-ple and change as we mature and grow. So, when we make the decision to marry, there is always a chance it will work or not work.

The constitution of marriage is honorable in the eyes of God, so we are excited about our journey together as husband and wife. However, we are completely aware that a success rate of 35 percent is lower in second marriages than a 50 percent success rate for first-time marriages. Admittedly, the thought of not making it is breathtaking. As we have continue to overcome challenges, I decided to share in this workbook some techniques that I employed as we dealt with them.

Starting this journey, I looked to the word of God for help to cope with the challenges and my feelings. When I opened the Bible, I began by looking for the requirements God had for wives. I tell you, I was going to find all of the reasons why my wife needed to change. See, I felt pretty good about myself, so it had to be her. It might sound funny but a lot of us make this same mistake.

Looking to the word of God opened my eyes to the fact that my feelings had little to do with my wife. The situation was really a lesson for me and an opportunity for me to grow in Christ. Immediately as I looked to God to find answers to support my position that my wife wasn't managing the situations the way I thought she should, the Lord began to show me myself and challenged me with questions. The questions started with: Do you love her like I love you? Are you giving yourself for her as I have given myself for you? Do you know I command husbands to love their wives as I love the Church (my bride) and to give themselves for them also as I have given myself for you, my Church (bride)? These questions silenced me and started me on a 7-day journey to gaining better understanding of some of my responsibilities as a husband.

As you go through this workbook, I pray you uncover your responses to the questions presented in the text and grow to understand the great mystery concerning Christ and the Church. Additionally, I pray that you are awakened to the reality that as husbands, we are called by God to look internally first to examine ourselves and our relationship with Him. Through that process, we become better men and husbands who love and cherish our wives as He does His Bride, the Church. Most importantly, I pray that you become better at being like Him: *The best bride's groom ever!*

DAY 1

The Commandment

Husbands, love your wives, even as Christ also loved the church, and gave himself for it [Ephesians 5:25].

Really, is this possible? What a commandment! Or even more, what a challenge from God—as if finding someone to love who will love you back is not hard enough. I know we can do all things through Christ who strengthens us; however, this is complicated, and even incomprehensible.

See, I believe most men would take a bullet for their wives out of sheer pride. However, that's no different than a gang member taking a bullet for a fellow gang member. So, giving yourself may not be hard when thought of in that context. On the other hand, giving yourself through a well thought-out plan that incorporates a level of suffering that you may not be able to measure by any standard than long-suffering is different. God planned to love us and gave himself for us with an understanding that it would require longsuffering on His part—longsuffering that would ultimately lead to the giving of His life upon the cross when we are so unworthy.

REFLECTION 1: Self-Sacrificing Love

Christ loved us so much that He had a well thought-out plan to give Himself to suffer the grief, misery, anguish and despair of the cross to save us from our sin (to marry us).

Can you think of a situation that you were not long-suffering? Explain what you could have done better.

_____

_____

_____

_____

_____

_____

_____

When I thought about my situation in comparison to the suffering Christ endured on the cross to save me, the challenges that I was facing seemed light. I realized that I needed to be more patient because my suffering seemed more like short-suffering instead of long-suffering in comparison.

Have you experienced suffering in your marriage that is equal to the suffering Christ endured that led to His being crucified by being nailed to the cross? Yes/No, please explain.

_____

_____

_____

_____

_____

_____

_____

REFLECTION 2: A Measure for Long-Suffering

When I thought of marriage, I never thought about calculating in a measure for long-suffering. For better and for worst? Yeah! In sickness and health? Yeah! For long-suffering that would lead to my feeling like I am dying (being crucified)? Nope! That was not part of the vows. A person being crucified by being nailed to a cross would welcome a quick death. Christ chose to endure it because He loves us even though we are not deserving of such love. Difficulties in our relationship with our wives can be very challenging because they test our love and patience. However, I don't know if they meet the definition for long-suffering in every case. I know some would beg to differ because when we are in that hard place in our relationships, it seems like the worst thing in the world. Remember, we needed grace and mercy, too.

Describe a time when you did not extend your wife the same measure of love and long-suffering that you received from God, even when you did not deserve it. Explain what you can do better next time.

_____

_____

_____

_____

_____

_____

_____

_____

Wow! When I realized God felt that way about me and He expected me to emulate the same love for my wife, I went and sat in a corner and repented. I thought to myself, man, you have a long way to go. I couldn't think of anything my wife did that was on the level of the crucifixion. I had to eat this large piece of spiritual food. Like a lamb led to the slaughter, Christ allowed mankind to torture and kill Him because he saw us as His bride and loves us enough to lay down His glory and majesty for the possibility at a relationship with us. Christ did not deserve it, yet He endured it. Sometimes we deserve the treatment we get from our wives because we are not faultless like God. The Lord is long-suffering and we don't deserve it; we need to extend the same grace and love to our wives.

Describe how you plan to handle situations that arise where you know you don't deserve the treatment you receive from your wife. Please explain below.

_____

_____

_____

_____

_____

_____

_____

_____

DAY 2

Vulnerability

After walking with the Lord for many years, we can look back and see clearly our track records are not the best. We have failed God many times on many levels. Yet, He continues to extend His hand to us to establish a relationship based on His love for us and with the hope we will develop a love for Him. This is a pretty big thing for God. He who is all powerful and all knowing, the creator of all things we know, places Himself in the vulnerable position where He is susceptible to our rejection. The Lord God opens Himself up to our criticism, dismissal and the possibility to be completely let down every time He extends Himself to us.

We don't have to be Bible scholars to notice that we continue to make mistake after mistake. Throughout biblical history, man continues to fall into idolatrous and destructive behaviors. Constantly, we are enticed and drawn away with lustful desires. Despite it all, God's love prevails and we find Him forgiving us and providing opportunities for us to continue in our relationship with Him. These opportunities are not without sacrifice and we can never forget God's expression of love to us by dying on the cross. He gave Himself for His Church or "bride" and now

He is looking to us as husbands to demonstrate the same level of love and sacrifice for our wives, our "brides".

REFLECTION 3: Service Your Wife Without Regard to Your Vulnerability

Husbands *must* have the capacity to extend themselves based on their love for their wives even though they might not get the same love in return. This is the true test of our faith in God because it places husbands in a seat of emotional vulnerability. For most men, this is difficult because it puts us in a position of possibly being rejected. Some husbands are not likely to chance that their acts of love will be ignored, dismissed or criticized. Some husbands find it extremely difficult to emotionally expose themselves because they do not want to experience the pain of rejection or being under-appreciated. This is equal to looking idiotic in a room full of strangers. The idea of looking stupid to their wives is breathtaking.

Christ is the greatest example for us in this situation. He never looks at us and wonders how we will respond to His acts of love. His focus is completely on Himself and how He feels about us. God's love is an outward reflection of His inward feelings about us. His expression of love is not predicated on who He is, but rather who we are to Him and how He feels about us. When God thinks about us, He loves us so much that He steps from His throne; lays down His crown and ego; and without regard to His being vulnerable, expresses His love for us. It is based on how He feels on the inside. When we face the vulnerable places in our relationship, we should look inward first. Start with the following question:

What do you think hinders you from extending love in the spirit of a servant to your wife as God has done for you? Explain below.

_____

_____

_____

_____

_____

_____

I struggled with this idea of just expressing love in spite of whatever I thought the outcome could be. I started to think of how I was going to express love to someone, knowing they might not love me back. Then, I started to duck and dodge the question by validating to myself that I was a desirable gentleman and surely some women would love me without my having to love them as Christ loves me. I was looking for the easy response, not the easy way. The bottom line is the idea of being vulnerable left me feeling very unsafe—so much so that I could not think rationally.

REFLECTION 4: Vulnerability is an Inside Job

I realized this wasn't about what anyone else could do to me. It is an inside job. It is completely about my heart towards God and if I could trust Him enough to be vulnerable. The fact of the matter is, my discomfort was truly about control or the perception of feeling you are in control. See, I grew to understand that vulnerability takes the control of the situation out of our hands and I disliked giving up control. This sounds crazy because it is! We never have control over what anyone does in response to what we do. We only have control over what we choose and do. So, another woman's love for me would not help because I still need to deal with me and my inability to believe God will not let me down, even in this situation. It is about getting to the place where I do what He says in spite of the unknown.

What is it you need to deal with inside of you so you can be vulnerable towards God enough to express love to your wife and trust God for the return? Explain below.

_____

_____

_____

_____

_____

_____

What do you think you need to address to move into the position of serving and loving your wife, not knowing if she is going to treat you well in return? Explain below.

_____

_____

_____

_____

_____

_____

What is your plan for addressing the obstacle? Explain below.

_____

_____

_____

_____

_____

_____

_____

In this situation, I began to realize my problem was not my wife. It was me. I had compartments in me in which I was happy to apply the Word of God and others that were exempt. *And whatsoever ye do, do it heartily, as to the Lord, and not unto men [Colossians 3:23]*. I was okay doing my job at work heartily as unto God because really, I knew there was a benefit attached to it; however, I was not applying God's word to all aspects of my marriage relationship because I could not see the benefit. I was focusing too much attention on how my wife would respond to my acts of love instead of how God would respond to my vulnerability. Through this process, I'm learning to trust God enough to be naked in my belief before my wife by expressing love based on my love for her without any guarantee that she will love me back. This place of vulnerability is new to me, so I must grow into it.

How do you think we benefit or profit from being vulnerable?

_____

_____

_____

_____

_____

_____

_____

It is not a simple thing, but my love towards my wife has to be a byproduct of my love towards God and a reflection of His life as He lives inside of me. I'm not trusting that my wife to reciprocate my love and service to her because my vulnerability is not towards her. My vulnerability rests with God, so I emulate His love and service to me in my relationships with my wife, trusting Him for the return. I love my wife through my love for God and His love for me. I'm vulnerable with my wife because the Lord is vulnerable with me and I'm trying desperately to be like Him.

When I am vulnerable before God and my wife, the benefits are trifold. My wife benefits from my relationship with God. My trust in God increases. I trust God to soften her heart for her to receive my love and service and to submit herself to Him as He operates in me. *Wives, submit yourselves unto your own husbands, as unto the Lord [Ephesians 5:22]*. Additionally, I gain the benefit of having a relationship with a submissive wife. When we allow God to reign in us as husbands by loving and serving our wives, we experience the byproduct of the honor and respect our wives have for God because they will love God in and though us. Our wives' expression of honor and service to God in us will be felt by us.

Additional Observations:

_____

_____

_____

_____

_____

_____

_____

DAY 3

One Flesh! — What About the Rest?

Therefore shall a man leave his father and his mother, and shall cleave unto his wife: and they shall be one flesh [Genesis 2:24 KJV].

The concept of being one in marriage is great. This is especially true when things are going as planned and there are no glaring problems in our marriages. It is easy to love when everything is lovely. Under these conditions, the honeymoon stage is full of wonders. We are excited about the future and what other great things lie ahead. During these times, the future turbulence that awaits every marriage is never thought of. Happiness is an aphrodisiac that causes us to overlook the fact that we are both human, and somewhere along the pathway to a healthy and thriving marriage, we are going to face challenges. If after the challenge we want to preserve our marriage, we will have to forgive one another and continue to move forward.

Since most men choose to only think on the good things, when challenges come, we are taken completely off guard and sometimes we find it difficult to forgive. I know I was not prepared for any challenges my wife and I would encounter in our marriage; however, my lack of preparation did not stop them from coming. When they came, I was not prepared to forgive my wife for the way we handled them and move on. Yes, I love my wife; however, forgiving her 70 times 7 *[Matthew 18:25]* was not incorporated into my marital plan.

On the other hand, in my relationship with God, I know that I'm going to test His love numerous times and stand in need of His forgiveness; without question, I know that He looks past my fault and forgives me. No matter how many times I do things that tests His love, He stays with me. Yet, when it comes to my relationship with my wife, I found myself wanting to hold a grudge against her and quickly forgetting that we are one flesh. I found myself shutting down and not talking at all. This would be what some call a form of the silent treatment. I once viewed this time as a break in communication. That could not be further from the truth. When we share our thoughts and ideas with one another, it is more than just communication—it is communion. Because of my unforgiving attitude, I allowed a breakdown in our communion, thereby inviting division into my relationship with my wife and creating a larger problem: a marriage that lacks the benefit of shared vision and spiritual purpose.

When we communicate with our wives, we are not just talking. We are communing, which is talking and interacting with intensity and intimacy. Communing with our wives is sharing things that we share with no one else but God. When we commune, we share possessions, responsibilities, and vision on a personal and spiritual level. There is an interchange/exchange of thoughts and feelings. Communion is deeper than basic conversation—it provides an opportunity for our wives to swap their thoughts and feelings on a spiritual level with our thoughts and feelings. During this interaction, our thoughts and feelings merge into one.

It is critical that we understand this. According to *Mark 10:8* when we marry, we become one flesh. The oneness occurs during the exchange of our vows before God and others. However, we have two components of our beings that remain separate from one another's. Our soul and spirit are still two separate parts of our beings. Our souls and spirits are not one with our wives' souls and spirits through marriage. It is through communing with one another that our souls and spirits come into agreement. Without communion, there is no agreement. Through marriage, we become one flesh; through communion, our souls and spirits become on one accord and find agreement.

REFLECTION 5: To Commune or Not to Commune

Do you have a set time to commune with your wife? Yes/No explain. If yes, explain some of the benefits you have encountered below.

_____

_____

_____

_____

_____

_____

_____

My wife and I have set Saturday mornings aside for our time to commune with one another. We always look forward to this time. In fact, we become pretty dysfunctional when we do not have this time together to share our thoughts and ideas and download from the week. We don't designate a set time, we typically talk within the window of time we have, depending on what we have on our calendars. We have talked for 30 minutes, 45 minutes, an hour and sometimes over two hours. We just sit on the bed and share.

Early in our relationship before we were married, we would go to breakfast together and share our feelings, thoughts and dreams. We would also talk about everyone jokingly while watching them, as if we were watching television. This was a time we set aside to bond with one another. This time spent with one another was one of the key elements in our relationship that brought us to marriage.

When commune time comes, do you take time to focus on you and your wife or are you distracted? Please explain below.

_____

_____

_____

_____

_____

_____

_____

During our communion, I realized that the focus of our time together changed from uplifting topics that strengthened our relationship to a time to focus on our challenges. We allowed our communion time to become polluted with discussions about our challenges. We both were distracted and our attention turned from the good things we enjoyed about one another to our difficulties.

When our focus changed, my desire to share intimate thoughts and feelings decreased. The challenges distracted me and I found myself shutting down more, little by little. I was not as sensitive or receptive of things my wife shared because I did not feel safe. I was preoccupied with the challenges. The intensity of our interaction that we experienced that originally brought us closer together became the intensity that fueled the challenges we were experiencing and began to cause a divide. Unfortunately, the same intensity we can experience in love can be experienced in the smallest conflict, making small things seem insurmountable. We could not get the problems out of our minds and out of our special time together.

We could only see the problems and not each other. Our vision of one another was blurred, which caused the spiritual vision for the household to become unclear, jeopardizing the oneness of our relationship. Neither one of us felt safe enough to engage in communion because we could not see one another, so we decided to limit that time. I would try to check out of the conversation before it became difficult. I did not think of my pulling away from that time as a break in our communion. Neither did I give any thought to the effect it could/would have on our relationship.

Have you ever decided to break communion with your wife? Yes/No, explain.

_____

_____

_____

_____

_____

_____

Was it a good decision to break communion? Yes/No, explain below.

_____

_____

_____

_____

_____

_____

_____

For me, in hindsight, breaking communion seems crazy because it is like making a conscious decision to stop communing with myself. Nevertheless, that is what I found myself doing. Since I'm one flesh with my wife, not communing with her is not communing with me. When I allow challenges to infiltrate and break down our communion time, I put us in a place of never being in complete agreement, spiritually or otherwise.

The fallacy is that we, like many other couples, keep the regular things going like sharing responsibilities and our material possessions because they are of a fleshly nature. Remember, we are one flesh, so the things that pertain to our flesh are easier to maintain, even though everything else may be falling to pieces. So to others, we appear like we are functioning normally and everything in our relationship is well when it is not! Things related to our souls and spirits become lacking because having no opportunity to commune means we cannot reach agreement between our souls and spirits.

This is very important to our marriage because our feelings, thoughts, dreams and ideas are products of our soul and spirit. No communion means the things related to our soul and spirit will be stifled. As married couples, we become *incapable of achieving anything spiritually* that will last or make a difference because we do not walk together in spiritual agreement. When we are not spiritually aligned, the household goes in two different spiritual directions and is divided. This can lead to a spiritual deficiency and miss direction of what God intended for the union. Also, the marriage will not mature in a state of togetherness but rather be at risk of one person growing at a rate that is different than the other. This is the equivalent of one of our legs growing longer and stronger, while the other leg remains weaker and shorter. It will become evident that your marriage is spiritually and natural out of sync when you try to move together as one in the spirit or when your souls are not prospering in unison. That is why God asked Israel the rhetorical question: *Can two walk together, except they be agreed [Amos 3:3 KJV]?* No! It is impossible!

REFLECTION 6: Spiritual Oneness

Being in one accord in our spirits puts us in unison with the direction that God provides for our marriages as it pertains to the kingdom and how we fit into His plan. If we cannot achieve oneness in spiritual things, we will not achieve God's purpose for our lives in our marriages. Sadly, God does not get the glory out of our union because we are spiritually in a state of disagreement.

Communion helps us learn how to walk together in the spirit in our marriages and to become spiritually aligned with Christ together. When this occurs, we hear the same thing because we are listening with one spirit, as God intended for the body of Christ: *[But God]...even when we were dead in sins, hath quickened us together with Christ, and hath raised us up together, and made us sit together in heavenly places in Christ Jesus [Ephesians 2:5 – 6].*

Have you wondered why you and your wife can't get along and be productive together with spiritual-related tasks? Explain an area of disagreement that needs your attention. How do you plan to overcome the obstacle?

_____

_____

_____

_____

_____

_____

Communion provides an opportunity for husbands and wives to become one in the spirit so we can accomplish God's purpose. Communion also provides the foundation for our souls to become aligned with one another's. The soul is the natural place of our mind, emotions and will. Through communion with our wives, we bring our souls into agreement also. It is important that we are thinking on the same track and that our wills or internal drives are in alignment. It is vitally important that we are on track with our thoughts and that our wills are fixed together, persistent and intent on achieving a common purpose. This will only happen through communion.

REFLECTION 7: Soul Mates

There are some unique situations where people find their soul mate. It's been said that soul mates understand and connect with one another in every way and on every level. These folks experience a sense of peace and happiness when they are with each other because they think each other's thoughts.

Well, that's not what happened in my marriage. You might agree that it is not the case in yours, also. Most married couples spend their entire marriages trying to agree—or if not, at least agreeing to disagree. This is our reality. In fact, one of the major attractions with some of us was that we have unique differences of opinion and really, at the end of the day, we love that about our spouses. That is not to discount the importance of us being able think alike with our desire systems. We can be different in a lot of ways; however, in order to achieve great things in life and in the Lord, we need to be in agreement on the things we are trying to accomplish in life and in the Lord.

It is important for our souls to be in sync; otherwise, one person will be trying to save money while the other one is spending it. One person will be preparing for the future while their spouse is only thinking only about today. One will be disciplined while the other will lack discipline because they are not working together to achieve the same vision. Having no communion leads to a divided marriage, where one person is walking in one direction while the other is running in a different one. This creates two different desire systems because no time has been set aside to exchange thoughts and feelings with each other.

Think of a time when you and your wife were not on the same page with the vision God showed you for the family. How did you deal with it?

_____

_____

_____

_____

_____

_____

_____

For me, when I realized we were not on the same page, I decided to stop sharing God's vision that He showed me for our family. My decision was partly based on my wanting to keep the peace and I figured that maybe one day she would see that God was with us. This was difficult for me because I felt like she did not trust that God could have a relationship with me. Also, I was confused because we could get on one accord when it came to the natural things like buying a home, but not when it came to the spiritual things. I was offended which led to my decision to break communion with my wife. See, I'm a preacher and teacher of God's word. I thought that my wife would see that I really love God and He loves me and that would be enough for her to trust that I was a man who was led by God. Well, it did not work that way. My feelings were hurt and I figured there was no reason to worry with it. I won't share the visions that God shows me, then I won't have to worry about being offended.

The Lord reminded me that a _prophet is not honored in their own country, or among their own kin, and neither in their own house_ [Mark

6:4 KJV]. Once I realized my expectations were not reasonable, I decided to correct my behavior. I could see I made a terrible decision. Immediately, I established a law with myself to never stifle or hold back God's vision for our marriage, because vision that is not shared is never realized. I was doing myself, my wife and the kids a disservice by allowing a break in our communion. I was blocking a blessing that only can come when my wife and I touch and agree in our souls and spirit. Remember, *that if two of you shall agree on earth as touching anything that they shall ask, it shall be done for them of my Father which is in heaven [Matthew 18:19 KJV]*.

In my quiet time, I meditated on how I would feel if the Lord stopped me from communing with Him. We all are guilty of not honoring the Lord as we should and not keeping Him first always. That is why *Mark 6:4* holds a lot of truth. Jesus could perform miracles everywhere else more than at home, where the people knew Him. Today, we limit God's ability to work in our lives based on our daily relationship that we have with Him. We honor Him differently today than we did when we were first introduced to Him because we are used to Him now. We put the Lord in the same position of deciding whether He should continue communing with us.

We should be grateful that He is not like us. He doesn't stop communing with us and sharing His vision for our lives with us. He is not easily offended because His knows us. He knows we are going to make improper decisions. It never stops Him from sharing with us and maintaining open communion with Him. We should be the same with our wives.

DAY 4

Looking Inward — Putting On Big Boy Pants

Looking inward is challenging. It takes humility and courage to take our eyes off of someone else to examine ourselves by asking hard questions, and even more to develop a response to those questions and implement change within ourselves. Only mature men are capable of this level of discipline because you cannot make a change to your behavior to fix a problem unless you first own up to the fact that you are part of the problem. Instead, most men deflect the blame and pin the problem on their wives.

The art of deflection is a natural instinct we all possess and have mastered. If we are good deflectors, we can create a diversion that takes the light off of us and place it on someone else. Sadly, we bring those same tactics into our marriages. The Lord is calling us to man up and put the big boy pants on! We can no longer be concerned about what our wives are doing/or not to the extent that we magnify those issues as a method to take the spotlight off of our poor behavior. Understand this: God is not easily distracted by our tactics. We need to focus on ourselves and make sure we walk according to His word because we cannot create a diversion for God. He sees through our tricks.

I, too, had to put on my big boy pants, sit at the table, and eat this meaty word. Oh yeah, that's right! I might as well put this out there. It might be difficult, and it requires looking inward and not at what you think your bride should be doing. Some are probably thinking "Well, she needs to do this..." or "She needs to that...." But I believe Ephesians 5:25 is for the man without any caveats or chaser. Husbands have to mature and take this one straight, like cough syrup without any Kool-Aid to wash the taste out of our mouths.

REFLECTION 8: Husbands Have No License to Withhold Love

Think about something your wife does that is completely wrong and every time she does it you respond to it negatively. Explain below.

_____

_____

_____

_____

_____

_____

_____

How does it make you feel after you respond negatively or ignore it?

_____

_____

_____

_____

_____

_____

_____

Do you hold onto it until later to bring it up in a conversation? Yes / No Explain below.

_____

_____

_____

_____

_____

_____

_____

I was the king of trying to hold onto a thought about something that my wife said or did that I felt rubbed me wrong. I would try to remember it and put it in my bag for the next conversation. Well, for me—as with most guys—this is crazy and it did not work. When the time comes for us to remember it, we forget it anyway. At least for me, I did not have the energy to recall it and place it into proper context with respect to the current conversation. I decided to not worry with holding onto the thoughts. Instead, I wanted to show her she was wrong by finding scripture to support my opinion of her. With that, I decided to focus on the clearly written scripture that was subject to little interpretation because I wanted it to be clear to her that she was out of order.

We all know that _Ephesians 5:22_ instructs: _Wives, submit yourselves unto your own husbands, as unto the Lord [KJV]._ You know we all have different definitions of what that looks like. Well, based on my definition, she wasn't as submissive as I thought she should be. So, for me, that meant I did not have to love and support her as much and it showed in my actions toward her. I felt that if you are not going to do right by me, you should not expect me to love you as much as Christ loves the church. That could not be further from the truth. Christ's love for the church is not contingent upon us doing right by Him. If it were, we would have been dropped from His list a long time ago. Truth be told, we fall into our sinful natures daily; we always stand in need of God's forgiveness and He forgives us. We make so many mistakes that you would think God's relationship with us is based on the number of times we do wrong and let Him down. Thank God for His grace.

Putting on big boy pants requires us to look at ourselves and take on the nature of God in spite of what our wives might be doing or not doing. Her perceived short comings are not a license to hold back love, long suffering, and forgiveness because the Lord never does that with us His love is consistent and constant. His grace is always sufficient, enough, appropriate for any level of sin, ample, abundant and adequate and our short comings are no challenge to His grace. It does not matter where we find ourselves outside of God's will; His grace is powerful enough to pull us back and wash us over and over again. God is calling us to emulate the same love towards our wives without compromise.

REFLECTION 9: Forgive as You Have Been Forgiven

Think of a time when you had the opportunity to forgive your wife that you chose not to forgive. How did it make you feel? Was non-forgiveness worth it?

_____

_____

_____

_____

_____

_____

_____

What result did it yield for you and your wife (what was the benefit)?

_____

_____

_____

_____

_____

_____

I don't see how not forgiving our wives can yield a positive interaction with our wives. Forgiveness is the primary key to acceptance. Our lack of forgiveness is received by our wives as a lack of acceptance. Most people want to be accepted and when they are not accepted, typically, they seek it from somewhere or someone else.

How would you feel about your wife seeking acceptance from somewhere or someone else?

_____

_____

_____

_____

_____

_____

_____

I see non-forgiveness as a two-edged sword. It cuts our wives and us, too. Understand that if we don't forgive, we go unforgiven of God our Father. *And when ye stand praying, forgive, if ye have ought against any: that your Father also which is in heaven may forgive you your trespasses [Mark 11:25 KJV].* I cannot afford to be in a state of non-forgiveness. I want to be acceptable to God, so I can't hold onto anything that will make me unacceptable. Besides, this is the equivalent of me not forgiving me because we are one, and that, my friend, is reckless.

What will you do differently next time when your wife says "I am sorry"?

_____

_____

_____

_____

_____

_____

_____

We cannot afford to take our eyes off of the sacrifice of God. He sacrificed His life and endured grave suffering on behalf of His bride, the Church. Because of His death, burial and resurrection, our sins are forgiven. It does not cost me anything that can be compared to His great sacrifice to forgive my wife. I should not try to make my wife pay retribution when she asks for my forgiveness because it costs me nothing to be in a position to grant forgiveness. I did not experience being beaten and nailed to a cross. I did not lay down my deity and humble myself to those who I created and let them take my life. It costs me nothing to accept my wife's apology when compared to the price God paid to accept mine. We, as husbands, need to lay aside our pride and forgive, just as Christ does for us on a daily basis.

REFLECTION 10: You Did Not Sacrifice Much – Why Should it Cost so Much for Your Forgiveness?

Pride, pride, pride! When we have such a high point of view or perspective of ourselves, we believe that others should pay homage to or respect who we believe we are. Some call it the male ego. I call it an unreasonable belief of our importance that make us feel superior to others, or in this case, to our wives.

The higher we think of ourselves, the less likely we will forgive others without wanting them to pay for our forgiveness. If our wives say they are sorry, it is not enough. We want them to feel pain instead of just forgiving them and giving them a pass. We want them to pay for the offense when Jesus already paid for all of our offenses. We want them to feel some type of emotional pain before we can say "I forgive you." If we make them pay for our forgiveness, it is not forgiveness. When we forgive someone, we bear the burden of the offense and take it off of them. Additionally, we free ourselves from being a victim and take the control back over our lives.

The misperception of non-forgiveness is that it makes us feel like we are in control when we have actually relinquished our control over to the offending person and the situation. We, in fact, become victims and if we are not careful, we will define our lives based on past hurts and offenses. The marriage is destined to fail and we are destined to fall because hurt people will hurt people—all because we are too prideful to let it go and move on.

That is why the Bible declares that *pride goes before destruction and a haughty spirit before a fall [Proverbs 16:18 KJV]*.

Think of a time when you wanted more from your wife than "I'm sorry" for an offense. What was driving your lack of forgiveness and need for her to pay for her infraction towards you?

_____

_____

_____

_____

_____

_____

What can you do differently next time?

_____

_____

_____

_____

_____

_____

Husbands, be careful, non-forgiveness is the reason why many people are sitting behind bars and living in jail cells. Non-forgiveness is like a cancer in our bodies that can grow completely out of control. Those who allow it to settle down and make itself at home in our relationships and in our hearts might as well turn themselves over to tormentors [Mathew 18:23-35]. It is a miserable feeling to have negative thoughts in our minds all of the time. We cannot allow non-forgiveness a place to rest in our marriages because it will block God's blessing on our unions.

Incomprehensible Love of God/Husband

In my efforts to understand God's love for us as His bride and how He has the same expectation for us, as husbands, to love our wives as He loves us [His Bride], for day 5, I put myself on the back burner just like God does with us, His bride, the Church. This was a challenge for me because remember, this is my second marriage. I really had high expectations for this relationship because we both are mature and experienced at being married. So, facing any challenges in our relationship within the first five years was hard to accept. Nevertheless, I set some criteria for a day of experiencing marriage from God's perspective of being married to us, "The Church," and how we put Him on the back burner as we go day to day.

Let's start by defining 'back burner'. Putting something or someone on the back burner means it or they are not important at the time. They will be considered sometime in the future when other things are not as important. During this self-imposed challenge, we must put our feelings on the back burner when we feel annoyed, offended, or underappreciated by our wives. When those feelings arise, we vow to put them on the back burner and remind ourselves that Christ forgives us, His bride, and in the same way, we too should forgive our bride and be available all of the time, just as Christ is available to us.

Husbands, I challenge you for the next 24 hours—when you experience feelings of annoyance, offense, or un-appreciation, think about the grace of God and how much of that grace you've exhausted due to your own actions toward Him. Just as you received forgiveness, forgive her and treat her like it never happened.

WARNING: This will be an eye opening experience and you are going to see how incapable you are of walking upright and flawless in God's sight. For me, I became aware of my own shortcomings and realized how much I need and rely on God for strength and forgiveness.

I challenge husbands to take the 24-hour challenge, but before you get started, you should ask yourself a few questions. It is important that you answer these questions before you begin the challenge and then again upon completing the challenge.

REFLECTION 11: The Back Burner Pre/Post Test

If the Lord looked at your wife through your eyes, would He see her or all of the problems you hold on too with respect to her? Yes/no, explain.

_____

_____

_____

_____

_____

_____

_____

When the Lord asked this question, I was embarrassed at my response. I realized that I was harboring some resentment towards my wife for not seeing things the way I thought she was capable of seeing them. Admittedly, I felt like she was giving too much power to forces outside of our marriage. I thought I was being patient but when I leveled with myself, I was tired of talking about the same challenges and it created a wall between me and my wife. Looking back in retrospect, I think my expectations for our relationship were so high that I could not embrace my wife's vulnerable moment because in every other situation, she was a tower of strength for me. Nevertheless, I was growing distant because when I looked at her, I saw the problem—not her.

I did not realize my vision became skewed, so at the time the Lord put this question before me, my response to the question was: Lord, I see a problem that I resented. This revelation broke my heart because I love her and I should never have allowed myself to go to this place; she deserved better of me as her husband. Besides, I would never want God to feel like that when He looked at me as a problem he resented.

When you look at your wife, do you see her or do you only see her flaws, mistakes, weaknesses, problems and issues? Explain below.

_____

_____

_____

_____

_____

_____

This is our second marriage. I approached this marriage with my eyes wide open. I knew the woman I married very well. I was aware of her strengths, weaknesses and areas in her life where she faced challenges. I chose to love her beyond those things. Besides, it was not bad and to keep it real, I had my own set of issues that I brought to the table. Even with my understanding of who my wife is, I found myself feeling different because of how I was being treated. Suddenly, things that did not bother me before became problems for me. My wife did not change from the women I married into someone else; rather, I was changing.

As the issues got more and more heated, this beautiful woman who I am deeply in love with started to look different to me. I was looking at her with the same eyes, but through a different lens. I looked at her through a lens that was clouded with the problems we faced and the flaws in our response to those problems. The challenges in our relationship were beginning to block our fellowship and intimacy.

The Lord looks at us, His bride, through His blood. His blood washes and cleanses us. He doesn't see our flaws, problems, issues and sins. They cannot block His fellowship with us because in His righteousness, we are made complete. The Lord's lens is a lens of His righteousness. When he looks at His bride, He sees himself.

When God looks at your wife, will He see you and Himself or your unforgiving spirit of condemnation?

_____

_____

_____

_____

_____

_____

_____

I know my wife and I are one flesh—*Therefore shall a man leave his father and his mother, and shall cleave unto his wife: and they shall be one flesh [Genesis 2:24 KVJ].* So, when the Lord looks at us, he sees me. However, I felt disconnected from my wife. I felt as if I were walking alone. Sometimes, we would revisit the difficult places and have extensive conversations about the same situations. The conversations never ended on a positive note. I tried to hold to my vow to love for better or worse. However, I found myself moving into a place where I was judgmental and disapproving. I was willing to forgive; however, it was based on her doing what I wanted at that time and that is not true forgiveness. If the Lord treated me like that, I would not be breathing right now. Nevertheless, that is where I was in my relationship.

When I realized I was judgmental, disapproving and offered forgiveness based on contingencies, I felt pretty low. My response was not good at all. I thought to myself, man, you are failing God's test with flying colors and it didn't matter to God because the questions continued to come.

If your wife stood before God today in judgment, would she be condemned based on the judgments you hold against her in your heart? Yes or No, explain how you feel about that?

_____

_____

_____

_____

_____

_____

This question was hard for me because generally, I would not want to see anyone condemned when they face judgment day. While pondering a response, I thought *WOW, the Lord is really questioning me about my feelings towards my wife.* I'm glad to say that I would never want my wife to face any form of condemnation, especially from God.

Now on the question of my own judgments (part two of the question), I could see where I was starting to judge her based on her actions but I was not holding my judgments in my heart. My love for God would not let me make those judgments a condition of my heart. She is my friend and partner in life and if she has no one else to go to, she has me. The thought of not providing her a safe place to hide is taking my breath as I write these words.

I realized after this question that I can never let challenges be the cause for destroying my marriage and relationship with my wife. My love for God and my wife must provide a transparent conduit between us and God. When the Lord looks at my wife through my eyes, I want Him to see my love for Him and my love for her; or in a real sense, my love for myself (she is me, see *Genesis 2:24*) as a direct reflection of His love for His bride, the Church.

God's forgiveness and care for His people is incomprehensible and it is a component of who He is. He forgives us and washes us with His word so that we can stand before Him without spot or blemish. We are able to stand without reservation or apprehension. In fact, we are told to come to Him boldly: *Let us therefore come boldly unto the throne of grace, that we may obtain mercy, and find grace to help in time of need (Hebrews 4:16 KJV).*

After every offense committed against Him, God removes all doubt and fear. We don't have to question whether He will be here tomorrow or next week. No doubt in our minds remains concerning whether He still feels the same way about us. We are free from wondering if He is still attracted to us, even though we gave into our lustful desires. God's heart remains soft towards His bride; He handles us gently and continues to implement the plan He has for our lives. He is patient, kind, and long-suffering. He does not see our sin when he looks at us. All He sees is His sacrifice of love. He looks at us through Himself because we belong to, and are part of, Him. **We are Him!** Because God loves Himself, He cannot help but love us too, because we are His. He bought us with His sacrifice on Calvary. As husbands, we should learn from His example and exercise the same with our brides.

REFLECTION 12: No Love for Yourself = No Love for Your Wife

By the time I got through Reflection 11 on day 5 of my 7-day journey, I felt completely broken and baffled at God's love. His love for his bride is incomprehensible because He loves us, His bride the Church, as He loves Himself. It is easy for Him because we are Him: N*ow ye are the body of Christ, and members in particular [1 Corinthians 12:27 KJV]*. God is okay with who He is and He loves Himself, so since we are His body, he loves us.

Do you love yourself [Yes/No]? Explain why.

_____

_____

_____

_____

_____

_____

_____

Do you have any personal insecurity that you need to address? If so, what are they and how do you plan to address them?

_____

_____

_____

_____

_____

_____

_____

The Lord is ok with being Alpha and Omega, the beginning and end. He loves Himself as the all-knowing King of Kings. The Lord's ability to love Himself is pure and He wants us to experience it. Since the Lord has the capacity to love Himself at such a high level, that gives Him the capacity to love His bride at a high level.

I examined my ability to love myself and found out that I loved me and I loved who I am and where I am in my life. I have not been perfect and everything has not gone as planned, but I am ok with myself. I love me and in my opinion, this makes me capable of loving others. In *Mark 12:30-31* the Lord gives us two commandments: *And thou shalt love the Lord thy God with all thy heart, and with all thy soul, and with all thy mind, and with all thy strength: this is the first commandment. And the second is like, namely this, Thou shalt love thy neighbor as thyself. There is none other commandment greater than these [Mark 12:30 KJV].*

Based on my evaluation, since I love myself, I have what it takes to love my wife as Christ loves the Church. I have known myself for over 40 years and have become acquainted with my strengths and weaknesses. I know what motivates me and what brings me down. So, I believed I was ready to love my wife with the same love I had for myself. Wow, was I wrong! I almost missed it. The scripture holds true—a person is only capable of loving someone else if they love themselves. What I almost missed is the fact that my love for myself was based on the person I used to be before I got married.

REFLECTION 13: Identity Crisis – Moving from Loving Me to Loving We [Me]

When examining the love I had for myself, I did not consider the obvious fact that I changed when I got married. I was applying the same love I had for myself when I was a single man to the new man I became when I married. That self-love is not sufficient for the new me I have become through marriage. My drawback was that I was in love with the old me. I did not realize that former single man changed when I became one with my wife through marriage.

The man that I just spent the last 40+ years learning about no longer existed in me. Now here I stand, looking in the mirror at a completely different person, albeit a new and improved me—a different me. Certainly I did not know much about this new guy. However, over the next few years, I would become acquainted with the new me and hopefully, learn about my new self and grow to love me—or in this case, WE!

Have you grown to love the new you who you have become through marriage? Why/why not? Explain.

_____

_____

_____

_____

_____

_____

_____

_____

_____

Do you think the new you is better or worse than the old you? Why/ why not? Explain.

_____

_____

_____

_____

_____

_____

I was a happy guy when I got married. I was thinking about marriage for better, definitely not worse so, when we hit a roadblock, I almost completely shut down in the relationship. I didn't know I was having an identity crisis. I did not like me or my wife at that time because I could not figure out who we were together. So, I did not like the new me. However, on the other hand, I knew I was better with my wife at my side. I just was experiencing the pains of getting acquainted with the new me. I mean really, if you put it into perspective, marriage is a surgical procedure in which two people enter as two separate, distinct people and come out as one. In _Matthew 19:6_, the Bible declares they are no longer two but one flesh.

Marriage is not an outpatient surgical procedure. Newly married people would really benefit from some overnight recovery time and physical therapy. In some cases, pain killers and muscle relaxers. We get none of that. We go from the marriage to the honeymoon and then face life head-on. We don't receive any medication or directions to make sure we heal together correctly. Recovery is on the fly and sometimes people heal and do well together as one. However, others experience serious problems that lead them back to the hospital for follow-up treatments. Through the process, some marriages develop scar tissue, which leaves unattractive marks. While learning to walk as one, they trip and fall numerous times, causing gruesome bruising and fractures that require the assistance of a cane or crutches. After many follow-up appointments and physical therapy, couples might learn to function well as one.

On the other hand, some couples come through the surgery of becoming one flesh not missing a beat. They understand what it takes to share the same mind and thoughts, and function in the same body together as a well-oiled machine. They embrace their new and improved selves and live together in harmony as one flesh. They love themselves even more together than when they were single and apart.

For me, I didn't know I was on a new journey to discovering how to love my new and improved self. I did not understand that when I got married, I changed who I am and she changed who she is. We became one, a merger of everything that I am with everything that she is. We are one flesh!

My mistake was trying to apply the principles of old loving to a new person. This would be the equivalent of putting new wine in old wine bags, and we all know Jesus warned against that [*Mark 2:22*]. I was trying to relate old ways of thinking into a new way of living when the foundational principles that my love for myself was built upon changed. My previous old love for myself was not big enough to accommodate the new me/we because there were some things about the new 'we' that I did not know about yet. The challenge is being patient enough to learn about the new attributes and benefits of merging our flesh with our wife's and becoming one.

A few years ago, I upgraded my surround sound system in my theater room. When I sat down to watch a movie, I realized I had about four remote controls for the different components. To turn the equipment on, I had to push the power buttons on each separate remote control. I had to search for one remote to increase or decrease the volume and another to start or rewind the movie on the blue-ray player. I found myself being a little annoyed as I fumbled with the remotes, but once the movie started, I was completely taken by the picture and sound quality. I was so impressed that my previous frustration with the remote controls was overtaken with joy.

In my frustration, I forgot that I absolutely expanded my home theater's capability to deliver professional, theater-like sound and picture quality. My quality of life was upgraded and I forgot to stop and think for a minute before getting frustrated. More remote controls meant more system components and capability. I needed to explore a solution to minimize the number of remote controls to just one. Later that day, after a little research, I purchased a new remote control with learning capability and now, I only need one remote control to turn the power off or on for all of the components with the push of just one button.

Sometimes, more challenges in marriage will lead to more blessings and benefits if we are patient enough to allow one another to become acquainted with our new selves and learn how to dwell together as one flesh.

List some of the benefits your wife brings to the marriage below.

_____

_____

_____

_____

_____

_____

_____

What can you do differently to make sure you benefit from them in the future?

_____

_____

_____

_____

_____

_____

_____

I learned there are some tangible and non-tangible benefits to joining my flesh with my wife's through marriage. I like the tangible things about my wife. Yes, I'm physically attracted to my wife and I can be physically intimate with her without reservation in the eyes of God. Additionally, I love her mind. She is my creditable sounding board. Then there is her kiss, which always feels like the first time we kissed— and I mean every time we kiss. My list can go on and on.

Then there are the benefits that come from God: *Whosoever finds a wife finds a good thing, and obtains favor of the LORD [Proverbs 18:22 KJV].* This means that husbands receive an attitude of liking beyond what is due from God. God has predetermined that He is going to respond to us in a positive manner because we have found a wife. The Lord has settled in His mind that He is going to have positive interactions with husbands. One thing I like about *Proverbs 18:22* is that it speaks of God's attitude of liking towards husbands and attitude is typically followed by behavior. It is God's behavior towards husbands that gives us the advantage in life. God's favor can cause us to be promoted above others when they are clearly more qualified for the job. In the eyes of many people this would not be fair but that is how God's favor works. His favor isn't fair, it causes the table to be turned to the benefit of the one's who believe in Him.

Have you noticed any situations since being married where you experienced God's favor at a level that you knew it could only be God?

_____

Admittedly, God rolled out the red carpet for my wife and me. We paid little to no money to move into our home; the home cost us almost half the price as some others in our neighborhood; and along the way, people were helping us achieve our goal of settling into our home. Without requesting it, people provided discount after discount. We have been extremely blessed because of God's favor.

I started with the material blessing because people tend to relate better to those. However, I cannot overlook the spiritual. *Marriage is honorable in all, and the bed undefiled: but whoremongers and adulterers God will judge [Hebrews 13:4 KJV].* We experience favor from God's judgment because we are not condemned for living a life as a whoremonger or adulterer. Also, marriage is honorable because it is symbolic of the relationship that Christ has with us, as His bride. But wait, there is more, although this next benefit is not as critical for me in my second marriage. It is still important to understand because it gives us perspective into the power of wives and the blessing that God has given us in them. Also, it helps us understand how God feels about us as His bride.

The benefit I am referring to is this: Through marriage, husbands get help that's meet for them. *The Lord God said, It is not good that the man should be alone; I will make him a help meet for him [Genesis 2:18 KJV].* In the Hebrew tongue, the two words that "help meet" are derived from are the Greek words "ezer" and the word "k'enegdo", meaning "help" or "salvation". So what this verse truly means is that our wives are our salvation.

What in the world? Originally, I could not wrap my thinking around this. Taking a closer look, I began to understand. Women provide a gateway to life. Without them, all mankind would not exist. I understand that my mother provided for me the ability to transform from my father's loins into a living breathing being by carrying me in her womb for nine months. I questioned, does that make her my salvation? No, that makes her my father's salvation. After he passes on, my father's seed [which is him] is saved in the world and continues to live through me. Actually, he never dies as long as his sons or daughters continue to have sons or daughters, but that cannot happen without a woman to carry the seed of my father and give birth to it into the world.

That is why our wives are opposites of us. They have different organs that enable them to become impregnated with the seed of man. Through this process, the wife becomes the salvation of her husband by giving birth to men or women of his seed. Sons and daughters who are born are the salvation or recovery of a husband's ability to live on through the lives of his children.

As the bride of Christ or the Church, we received salvation from God. On the other hand, after becoming saved people of God, we become God's salvation in the world. *Matthew 5:13* declares that we are the salt of the earth. That's why we have this great commission from God to go and make disciples: *Praising God, and having favor with all the people. And the Lord added to the church daily such as should be saved [Acts 2:47 KJV].* Christ continues to live on through us, His bride [wife], as we convert the world to His likeness and image by adding people to body of Christ.

Our wives become us through marriage and together with us; they preserve our seed and life in the earth. They are a treasure to us and should be treated as such. I give thanks daily for the blessing of having a wife.

DAY 6

Communication

What would we do if we could not communicate with our God? I believe the songwriter put it best in saying they would be like a ship without a sail. In relationships, communication is one of the major building blocks to intimacy. If we could not communicate through prayer with God, we would not feel connected to Him. A lack of communication is the cause of many breakdowns in marital relationships. This critical element cannot be overlooked. If it is overlooked, however, I can almost guarantee you your marriage will not last.

God communicated His love to us, His bride, in that while we were yet sinners, he died for us. Now He is challenging husbands to take that same position in our love for our wives. We can look to God as a good example of what communication with our wives should be.

Communicating with our wives during good times can be challenging, so we all know how uncomfortable communicating is when problems become the topic of our conversation. Most men that I know would rather find a corner to sit in by themselves than to endure the difficulties of perplexing conversation. I say that with a smile on my face because I experienced many difficult conversations that left me feeling defeated. It is hard to talk to our wives when they have experienced disappointment, especially when we are the reason for their disappointment. It can be even more challenging when they are disappointed and we have no power or influence over the people involved, yet we are receiving all of the punches as if we do.

Think of a conversation you had with your wife because of something someone else did that had nothing to do with you. Explain how you felt?

_____

_____

_____

_____

_____

_____

_____

Even though you had no power to do anything to fix it, what could you have done differently?

_____

_____

_____

_____

_____

_____

_____

I recall hard conversations with my wife about some of my family members and their actions. I did not agree that they intended to bring an offense; however, what I learned was that particular point was not the issue. It did not matter what their intentions were and whether they had malice in their hearts or not. I should have responded differently. First, I should have acknowledged and validated my wife's feelings, not whether I agree or disagree. Secondly, I should have understood that she is entitled to feel the way see feels.

I guess you figured out by now that I did not do either of the two things I mentioned. Instead, I did what most men do: I focused on fixing the problem. I went into an investigative mode to uncover who did what and what I needed to do to fix it. Quickly, I realized I'm not capable of fixing all problems. In my case, I wanted to address whoever brought the perceived offense when I needed to start with making sure my wife knows she has the liberty to feel the way she feels about whatever happened—not that she is right or wrong for feeling what she feels. I should have communicated to her that as my bride, she is entitled, and has the liberty, to feel whatever kind of way she feels about whatever.

Think about it—we are okay with ourselves when we perceive different things about the way people act towards us and others. Well, our wives are us because we are one flesh. So, we should be okay with whatever conversation they want to have with us about whoever they want to talk to us about.

What if God limited us to certain topics and people who we could talk to him about? Explain how you would feel?

_____

_____

_____

_____

_____

_____

_____

Do you have a list of topics that are off limits for your wife to talk about? If so/not, explain why?

_____

_____

_____

_____

_____

_____

_____

Do you have a certain people in your life that you prefer your wife to not talk about? If so/not, why?

_____

_____

_____

_____

_____

_____

I did not have any topics or people who were off limits in our conversation; however, I think my wife thought I did. After realizing I did not, we proceeded forward with uninhibited conversations. This was a major step because it opened the lines of communication. We speak freely on any topics or any feelings we have about anyone in our families, our coworkers, our children, etc.

I don't know about you, but I would not be happy—nor would I want to maintain a relationship—with someone who I had to walk on egg-shells with every time I needed to talk to them. The Lord allows us to have a meaningful exchange of information with him and when we conclude our conversation with Him, we walk away knowing He heard us; understands our feelings; and more importantly, we believe He is going to do something on our behalf.

Our wives should be able to take comfort in knowing that our ear is always opened and we are going to do everything to understand them and fight on their behalf. Even when we are offended by their words, they should know we are still here for them. Even if they find themselves in sinful situations, they should know they can come back to home-base with us and feel safe without fear of judgment. Husbands must always convey the message to our wives that they have a place to belong and we accept them in whatever state they find themselves.

REFLECTION 14: Convey Acceptance

Communicating to our wives acceptance through difficult times is not the easiest thing to do. Typically, we experience pain when we are offended by our wives. The pain is greater with our wives because they are very close to us. Sometimes we categorize offenses, making some acceptable and others un-acceptable. For example, we all know that bringing an offense by committing adultery is the hot button that can void our marriage contracts. However, some people decide to forgive those offenses and continue in their marriages. Others feel that the offense of adultery is too egregious to continue in the relationship and move past. However, anything short of that, God expects husbands to forgive and accept their wives.

Forgiving takes a lot of humility but to open your heart and mouth to convey a message of acceptance on the heels of being offended is taking it to the next level. It is nice when husbands stand with arms opened wide to receive our wives after an offense and I'm sure that makes them feel really good. However, words of affirmation, spoken in the right tone, coupled with positive body language strengthen our wives back to their place of belonging.

Do you forgive your bride daily and wash her with your words of affirmation to strengthen her? Yes/No, Explain.

_____

_____

_____

_____

_____

_____

_____

The Lord washes us from our sin and cleans our hearts so they long after Him. He tells us He will never leave us or forsake us *[Hebrews 13:5]*. He will never see us begging for bread. Even after we make big mistakes and fall out of God's grace, He stands with His arms stretched wide telling us to come on back home. The Lord affirms us and lets us know that He has us and we are safe in His arms.

One day, after having an intense conversation, I noticed a wall was building up between me and my wife. It seemed like the wall height increased with each additional conversation. We would talk and walk away knowing that we felt indifferent towards one another. Initially in response, I laughed at our stubbornness because neither one of us wanted to call uncle nor let the problem go. We could not just talk about it and let it go. We had to carry it around and let our feelings fester into something worse.

Through this exercise, I realized that carrying the poisons of the conversation around in our thinking allowed insecurity to set in. I noticed my wife was drawing away. Like anyone else, she was trying to protect herself because she thought I was going to choose someone else over our marriage. This was disheartening because I was not carrying un-forgiveness, yet I was experiencing the fruits of un-forgiveness.

Upon examination of myself, I realized that I neglected to wash my wife of the poisons with my words of affirmation to strengthen her confidence that she is still accepted and loved. With that, I went to her and told her that I'm here with her to stay. I love her and I will always choose my side, which is our side. I wanted her to know that she is my partner and I'm with her until the end. It is us against the world. I washed her thinking with my words of affirmation and then she understood that I accept her and still love and want her. It was then that she understood that I want our marriage and that I am intentional about making it work.

Can you think of a time when you chose someone or something over your wife (yourself)? Explain how you felt afterwards and if you think it was the best decision.

_____

_____

_____

_____

_____

_____

_____

_____

The Lord provides a great example for us. He is very clear with us about His intentions for us to have a successful relationship with Him. His deliberate actions led Him to endure suffering on our behalf, so that we might experience eternal life with Him as His bride. Also, He provides us grace and mercy whenever we make a mistake. I'm grateful that each day, we are provided the grace and mercy to start anew. The Lord does not hold our sins, mistakes, offenses or short-comings over His bride's [us] head. In fact, He chooses to never remember our faults. His kindheartedness towards us is purpose driven to achieve the result of maintaining a loving relationship with us. If He held us accountable for each and every sin or offense, we would be consumed [dead]. The Bible declares: *It is because of the LORD's mercies that we are not consumed, because his compassions fail not. They are new every morning: great is thy faithfulness (Lamentations 3:22-23 KJV)*.

The Lord chooses to be compassionate, kind and understanding with regards to us. He continues to communicate to us His commitment and desire to spend the rest of His life with us. The Lord is so serious about this that He provides new mercies each and every day.

Why does the Lord provide new mercies every day? Yes/No, Explain.

Why should we provide new mercies to our wives each day? Yes/No, Explain.

_____

_____

_____

_____

_____

_____

_____

This was difficult for me to wrap my thinking around. I struggled with this. Not with the idea of needing new mercy—more with the idea that my wife needs new mercies each day and how and when it would be applicable. Originally, I responded to this question with a question. After meditating on the question, the Lord provided revelation.

My wife and I work approximately 4 miles apart; however, we decided that it is more beneficial for us to commute to work in separate vehicles because it provides us with the much needed freedom to manage our day at work. However, during the summer months, we decided to commute to work together a few days of the week. What I realized during those days is that we have different concepts of time. On some occasions, our different definitions for being on time would lead to my waiting outside of my sweetheart's place of employment for her to come down to go home. It was one of these times when I had to wait for the third or fourth time that I found myself saying, "Wow, why can't we leave on time!" At that point of becoming frustrated and slightly annoyed, I understood why new mercies are necessary. New mercies are needed when the same mistake is made over and over again. New mercies take the power out of old mistakes and convey our intent of being committed to our wives. New mercies make the same mistake a new mistake every time we make it over and over again.

REFLECTION 15: Conveying Commitment – Longevity

The Lord applies new mercies when we make the same mistake over and over again. I was getting tired of my sweetheart running behind on time because I felt like it was a reoccurring problem. However, when I applied a new mercy to the old problem, I immediately felt better and she never experienced any of my frustration because my new mercies made the old problem a first time offence. We all know in most court cases, the first-time offense is typically excused by most people. The lesson I learned is that old mercies do not work on old problems. Old mercies grow tired and run out. They are limited in their ability to cover mistakes that we continue to make. I don't know about you but I run out of fingers to count on both hands the number of repeat offenses I have made. Thank God for new mercies for old mistakes.

The Lord never sees our repeat offenses as repeats. They are always viewed as first time offenses because we are given a clean slate after every time we make mistakes. See, it is easy to stay on the honeymoon when new mercy is applied because every day is new—because we don't give space for grudges to grow and fester into problems that create walls of division. The Lord provides us with a never-ending honeymoon because every mistake we make is like the first. He chooses to forgive and forget our mess every time.

Do you approach each day with her as a clean slate and opportunity to explore different ways to strengthen the relationship? Yes/No, Explain.

_____

_____

_____

_____

_____

_____

_____

Do you see her without spot or blemish or do you see her through a clouded lens of un-forgiveness? Yes/No, Explain.

_____

_____

_____

_____

_____

_____

Do you extend new mercies daily? Yes/No, Explain what could you do differently to get better?

_____

_____

_____

_____

_____

_____

_____

I resolved to live my relationship with my bride starting every day with a clean slate, just like God does for me. I'm still working on adjusting my spirit to delete history because every day God treats me like I did not make the same mistake just the day before. This is very difficult; typically, we want a person to wallow in their wrong deeds when we need to be Christ-like and let it go. He provides new mercies for me, so I should do the same with my bride.

Do you find yourself sometimes wanting to hold on to un-forgiveness? Yes/No, Explain.

_____

_____

_____

_____

_____

_____

_____

How will you address those feelings when they occur again?

_____

_____

_____

_____

_____

_____

_____

I found myself recently struggling internally with forgiving my wife for the way she treated me. This is classic of God—to give revelation to us and immediately, we make the proclamation that we have learned how to walk in that newly-found revelation. Then, here comes the test.

When the test came, the Lord reveled to me that I have some issues that I need to resolve within myself. I found that I struggle when I feel like the treatment was not merited. When I did not demonstrate any behavior that would suggest you should be disrespectful or mean to me. When that happens, I really wrestle with forgiving my wife and acting as if it did not occur. My feelings were standing in the way of the clean slate theory. I had to come to grips with it. When I encountered these situations, I knew I needed to have a conversation about the events that transpired—not necessarily to point a finger to place blame, but more as a lesson in the proper way we should treat one another. My wife and I have a saying that we both agree on: we teach people how to treat us. That applies to us also and the way that we treat one another.

Reality hit me in my face. I thought I had this one mastered until I was really treated like Christ. *He was oppressed, and He was afflicted, yet He opened not his mouth; He is brought as a lamb to the slaughter; and as a sheep before her shearers is dumb, so He openeth not His mouth (Isaiah 53:7 KJV)*. I admit I'm still growing in grace to be more like Christ. Jesus provided another great example of His power to humble Himself and set the bar high for us to aspire to.

REFLECTION 16: Convey Gratitude

I have been walking with the Lord since September 1985 and He has been my best friend ever since. I cannot think of a time over the last fourteen years that He was ever sad to see me coming. I know this might sound crazy but the Lord always shows appreciation for the time I spend with Him. I don't understand it, He has blessed me to be who I am and He loves me for being the person He made me to be. When I come into His presence singing songs of praise or writing articles that are love letters to Him, He expresses His love and gratitude to me for being a recipient of my love and resting place of my affection. He has made me all that I am and I understand I would not be here if not for His grace—so really, I owe my love and dedication to Him. However, He doesn't treat me like I owe Him. He conveys His gratitude towards me and lets me know that His love for me runs deeper than my imagination.

The Lord appreciates me for choosing to love Him and His affection for me is unmatched. I don't understand how a God so great shows gratitude for me being affectionate towards Him. He makes Himself available to me whenever I call. He loves me without limitations and ultimately, He gave Himself as a sacrifice and continues to give Himself on my behalf. He forgives all of my faults in spite of my inconsistent ways, my not so lovely attributes, and my sinful nature, which stands at the doorway waiting for an opportunity to offend Him. He looks at me with love in His eyes and conveys to me His gratitude for me having a mind to receive all of His love and affection. He loves me and will not allow anything to separate me from His love.

Are you grateful to have your wife in your life? Yes/No, explain why.

_____

_____

_____

_____

_____

_____

_____

Does your wife know how thankful you are to have her in your life? If yes, how do you express it? If no, what can you do different to show her? Explain below.

_____

_____

_____

_____

_____

_____

_____

I know I can do better at conveying appreciation and gratitude to my wife. I can do this by making sure I give her my undivided attention when she wants to talk or share. I can provide emotional support by being present when she needs me. Also, I can listen to her when she needs to talk about things, without judging her for her thoughts and actions. We all know that gifts communicate gratitude and yes, we can always do better at that. I think I do some of these things; however, I will benefit from a tune-up.

REFLECTION 17: Conveying Inseparability

Inseparable—wow, what a concept! Most marriages today are not entered into with the mindset to be inseparable. We like the concept and idea of inseparability; however, when turbulent times come, we are ready to move on to the next relationship with fervor. I think we forget that through marriage, we become one flesh with our wives and separating flesh from flesh is very difficult. It is a little trickier than just determining who gets what from the marital estate. It is a very pain-staking operation, typically met with opposition from one of the people going through the process. God is the only one who can divide without causing grave pain and He hates divorce *[Malachi 2:16]*.

It is much better to take on the mindset that we are in it until death do us part. My wife and I say, *Ride or die, baby!* Maintaining a love that does not change when the wind blows or when we make mistakes is not easy. A love which adjusts and expands to cover offenses against one another is built over time. *And above all things have fervent charity among yourselves: for charity shall cover the multitude of sins [1 Peter 4:8 KJV]*.

Love covers all. I once held the opinion that if you love someone enough, they will respond. What I have learned as a husband is to just love—period. I cannot focus on my wife's response to my love; she will have to give an account for that. It is not for me to judge. In this case, it goes back to being vulnerable enough to trust God, take Him at His word and walk in it. Husbands must learn to yield their trust over to God and have faith in His word.

As the bride of Christ, we are inseparable because His love covers our mistakes, shortcomings, sins, etc. He never seeks a divorce from us because He never sees us as being unattractive, unworthy, or undesirable. That is because He only sees His love that covers our sins. He clothes us with His love and that is the lens He chooses to see us through. The Lord never sees the nakedness of our sins and mistakes; He always sees us clothed with His love and righteousness. Note: I said His love and righteousness. Not ours. The Lord is calling husbands to a higher level of love. Since we have no righteousness, all we can cover our wives with is our love.

Have you clothed your wife with your love or is she naked and her flaws exposed? What could you do differently?

_____

_____

_____

_____

_____

_____

_____

We are almost at the end of this workbook and finally, we come to a question that I feel pretty good about. My wife and I are pretty private and we don't share a lot of our personal information with others. So, with that, I always knew that sharing personal things and situations with others would be considered a major breach of our trust. Also, I realized some time ago that I'm in no way perfect, so I can't look at my wife as if I have no spots or blemishes. In fact, I look at her through the eyes of my brokenness. I know that I have nothing to glory in but God. I'm striving and trying to make it to heaven and I continue to fall and get back up, so I cannot expect her to always get it right. So, I look at my wife through a lens of love and brokenness, realizing that we are both recipients of the grace of God, and we are both striving to make heaven. If I continue to look at my wife through a lens of my love for her and with a surrendered heart that has yielded control to God, we will be inseparable.

I love the way the Apostle Paul questioned the saints of God. In _Romans 8: 35- 39_, the Apostle Paul asks the most wonderfully stated rhetorical question: _**35** Who shall separate us from the love of Christ? Shall tribulation, or distress, or persecution, or famine, or nakedness, or peril, or sword? **36** As it is written, for thy sake we are killed all the day long; we are accounted as sheep for the slaughter. **37** Nay, in all these things we are more than conquerors through him that loved us. **38** For I am persuaded, that neither death, nor life, nor angels, nor principalities, nor powers, nor things present, nor things to come, **39** nor height, nor depth, nor any other creature, shall be able to separate_ *us from the love of God, which is in Christ Jesus our Lord [KJV].* We know the answer is nothing. God's love will prevail for us—period. He just loves His bride that much! INSEPARABLE!

Is your love for your wife as deep as God's love for you that it is inseparable? If not, what adjustments can you make to develop the same love for her?

_____

_____

_____

_____

_____

_____

_____

The million-dollar question: when you look at your wife, DO YOU SEE YOU?

_____

_____

_____

_____

_____

_____

I pray that by this time, your answer to this question is YES.

DAY 7

The Wrap-up:
What I Learned...

I know you are wondering how I made out by the end of the 7 days. Well, what I found is that there are many opportunities for my wife to offend me and if we stay together, we will offend one another along the way. However, her offenses to me are no different from those that I commit against her and God by co-mission or omission. So, I learned to give the same level of forgiveness to her that I receive from God when I make mistakes. Additionally, I noticed that for many situations in which I felt offended, typically, it was just my perception. Most of the time, I was over responding to something I perceived as offensive; however, after taking a second look, I realized my response was not merited.

As I examined my response to my wife, I started to look closer at my offenses before God. First of all, I noticed that when I offend God, it is not a perceived offence. It is a true offense, which I deserved to receive God's hand of correction for; however, the Lord forgives me time after time. With that, I began to pay more attention to the number of times I offended God in my daily walk. By the end of each day, I felt pretty humbled because I was worse at offending God than my wife could ever be at offending me. This humbling realization brought me to my knees and to a state of brokenness before God.

I realized that on my best day of consecration, my righteousness is a filthy rag. I have no righteousness without the provision of salvation afforded me by Christ. Therefore, I came to the understanding that I must maintain my heart in a state of brokenness and surrender. I must remain broken before God and my wife. I have learned that the sacrifices of a broken and contrite spirit cannot be despised by God *[Psalms 57:17]*.

I was awakened to the fact that I am not the best communicator with my wife. My actions are not always clear and received by her as deliberate. I learned that I must be a better communicator of my intentions and commitment to my wife and our marriage. When communicating, I must always have an open heart and ear to hear my wife's heart. Just as God is gentle and loving with me and hears me when I call, I must be the same with my bride. He never throws me away and is always there for me, so will I strive to be there for her.

Through this process I found myself seeking God's grace and mercy. Also, I found an overwhelming level of gratitude to God for His provision and forgiveness in my life. He is my salvation. So, for me to love as Christ loves, I must be a conduit of salvation and a place of safety that through my love and long-suffering, my wife can see Christ in me.

I was introduced to what it means to be vulnerable enough to trust God without knowing the answer to this question: If I extend love to my wife, would she trample it underfoot or embrace it and give love back to me. It is very risky to put yourself in a place of loving someone as Christ loves us when there is no guarantee that they will love you or appreciate your demonstration of the love of God. Yes, if asked, most women would respond that they would love to be loved by their husband at the same level that God loves each individual. However, when they are granted that opportunity, they might not trust that the person is genuine; they might feel convicted and become defensive or judgmental. They even might view your expression of love as weakness because they feel you are too forgiving and loving. I still challenged myself to walk it out. Weakness would be deciding to take the easier route of not trying to be as Christ. I also learned that it takes a lot of inner strength to walk in the shoes of Jesus Christ.

Thank you for taking this journey with me.

I can't guarantee that this approach will work for every marriage. I can guarantee that as you implement the teachings of this workbook, you will find out who you are and what you are made of. I pray that your journey through this workbook has been enlightening and that you have drawn closer to God and your wife. The Lord continue to bless you and cause His face to shine upon you. Amen

www.ingramcontent.com/pod-product-compliance
Lightning Source LLC
Chambersburg PA
CBHW071633040426
42452CB00009B/1607